VIRTUOUS

VIRTUOUS

A Study for Ladies of Every Age

NANCY WILSON

Published by Canon Press
P.O. Box 8729, Moscow, ID 83843
800.488.2034 | www.canonpress.com

Cover design by James Engerbretson
Interior design by Valerie Anne Bost
Printed in the United States of America.

Library of Congress Cataloging-in-Publication Data

Names: Wilson, Nancy, 1952- author.
Title: Virtuous : a study for ladies of every age / Nancy Wilson.
Description: Moscow : Canon Press, 2016. | Includes bibliographical references and index.
Identifiers: LCCN 2016026746 | ISBN 9781591281955 (pbk. : alk. paper)
Subjects: LCSH: Christian women--Religious life. | Christian women--Conduct of life. | Virtues--Biblical teaching.
Classification: LCC BV4527 .W5555 2016 | DDC 248.8/43--dc23
LC record available at https://lccn.loc.gov/2016026746

16 17 18 19 20 21 22 23   10 9 8 7 6 5 4 3 2 1

CONTENTS

PREFACE

This is a small group of lessons on Christian virtues that I have used to lead Bible studies for junior high, high school, college aged, and older women. It seems to me that if God wants us to be diligent in adding virtue to our lives, it is helpful and necessary to give thought to what that means. So I have isolated some biblical virtues in order to discuss what the Bible says about each one, and I have included some thoughts on application to help us grow in our understanding of each topic. Over the years women have asked me for help in leading small group studies. I hope this little collection will also be of use for that purpose, so I have included some discussion questions for guiding your interaction. I suggest you go over all the Bible verses and text of each chapter together as a group, discussing as you go. Then when you have finished, you can turn to the discussion questions at the end of the chapter. These particularly target application. You may find that you have already discussed these things as you went through the chapter, and other questions may occur to you. You are bound to notice that some verses appear more than once. That's simply because they apply to more than one virtue, so I have referred to them accordingly.

> But also for this very reason, giving all diligence, add to your faith virtue, to virtue knowledge, to knowledge self-control, to self-control perseverance, to perseverance godliness, to godliness brotherly kindness, and to brotherly kindness love. For if these things are yours and abound, you will be neither barren nor unfruitful in the knowledge of our Lord Jesus Christ. (2 Pet. 1:5–8)

This exhortation in 2 Peter is what first prompted me to think about what it means to be actively pursuing virtue. If we are increasing in these things the apostle mentions, he says the result is fruitfulness in the knowledge of Christ. So this is the best kind of endeavor for all Christian women. Our goal is to grow in our faith and love for God. My prayer is that this little study will help us get there.

I

WHAT IS VIRTUE?

Women of all ages sometimes struggle with understanding their calling and purpose in life. But God has a good purpose for each one of us. In this short book we are going to look at one important aspect of the calling of every Christian, and that is to be diligently engaged in adding virtue to our lives. A virtuous woman is a woman who exhibits godly character traits. So virtue is about ethical behavior, and it's about our character. The outside (the good things we do) must spring from what's inside, and those two must be consistent. If we are trying to "be good" without a godly character, we won't be able to keep it up for long. But if we have been renewed by the Holy Spirit in Christ, we will necessarily work out what He has worked in. Of course it is possible for a person who has received grace and forgiveness to start to slide. Therefore, we are to *pursue* virtue and not just assume it.

Feminine virtue includes a toughness that we may not normally associate with it. Boaz told Ruth, "All the people of my town know that you are a virtuous woman" (Ruth 3:11). This word "virtuous" is the feminine equivalent of a Hebrew phrase translated "man of great wealth" (*Geneva Study Bible*). In other words, a woman with this kind of reputation has influence and moral authority; she has standing in her community. She is a woman of stature. We might think of some of the "leading women" of the community referred to in Acts 17:4, who "joined Paul and Silas." And Proverbs 12:4 says that "An excellent wife is the crown of her husband." An "excellent wife" is translated literally as "a wife of valor." So I think we can safely say that all virtue must include a manly kind of courage. Women would do well to think of themselves in this way, rather than assuming that a virtuous woman is a retiring, Victorian stereotype who shrinks away from getting her hands dirty.

Virtues are good qualities that God's Word defines for us. In the world, some virtues may fall out of favor, and unbelievers can call evil good and good evil. But for the Christian woman, life is much clearer. God's Word is straightforward and not subject to fads and shifts. So let's consider a few Scriptures that teach us about the pursuit of virtue.

Our Biblical Texts and a Little Commentary

Paul tells us in Philippians to find some virtue and think about it: " . . .if there is any virtue and if there is anything praiseworthy—meditate on these things" (Phil. 4:8). Virtue must be a good thing; it must be praiseworthy or we would not be commanded to fill our mind with it. Finding out what is virtuous is a worthy endeavor, and we should therefore be pleased to undertake the study of such a topic.

Not only are we *to think* about virtue, we are to diligently *pursue* it.

> But also for this very reason, giving all diligence, add to your faith virtue, to virtue knowledge, to knowledge self-control, to self-control perseverance, to perseverance godliness, to godliness brotherly kindness, and to brotherly kindness love. For if these things are yours and abound, you will be neither barren nor unfruitful in the knowledge of our Lord Jesus Christ. (2 Pet. 1:5–8)

We are to add virtue to our faith. When we are active Christians, giving ourselves to the pursuit of holiness, God has promised that we will be fruitful in our Christian lives.

But we have to be able to say that these things really are ours, and that we have them in abundance. We can't expect God to bless us the same way if our lives are characterized more by vice than by virtue. No, if we overflow ("abound") with virtue, He will make us bear fruit.

It is of primary importance for us to know and remember that *He is the One* making us fruitful. It is not we ourselves who accomplish this. "But by the grace of God I am what I am, and His grace toward me was not in vain; but I labored more abundantly than they all, yet not I, but the grace of God which was with me" (1 Cor. 15:10). Paul brags that he has worked harder than all the other apostles. But he is quick to add, "Yet not I, but the grace of God which was with me."

If we think we can just enroll in a program to attain virtue and get a diploma in a few months, we are seriously mistaken. Without the grace of God, none of our labor is worth anything. So as we go through and discuss each of these virtues, we must be keenly aware that our pursuit of holiness is all of grace or it is nothing at all. In fact, it is less than nothing. Without God enabling us to study, to pray, to think about these things, to work to apply what we learn, nothing will happen. This will be a waste of time. But if we believe that He works in what we then work out, if we apply ourselves to be diligent to learn, then He has promised to bless us more abundantly than we can imagine. This is where our faith is put to work. We pursue godliness, trusting that God will by His Spirit do far more than all we can ask or think.

I have rounded up a handful of biblical qualities that we could call virtues. I do not pretend that this is an exhaustive list! Far from it. Even as I assembled this, I thought of more. This collection is just to get us started.

In all these things God is central. He is the only One who is truly holy and virtuous, and He calls us to imitate Him. This would be impossible had He not sent His Son to redeem us and make us new creatures. And then He gives us His Spirit so we can obey Him. Pursuing virtue is all about God from start to finish.

QUESTIONS

1. What qualities come to mind when you think of the word "virtue"?

2. How do we meditate on virtuous things? When do we meditate on virtuous things?

3. What prevents us from pursuing virtue?

4. What things distract us from a virtuous life?

5. What does the world hold to be virtuous? Can you think of some virtues the world holds dear that are consistent with biblical living? Some that are not?

2

DILIGENCE

Diligence means working hard and putting care and effort into your work. It means constant, careful effort, not just working in spurts and starts but persevering in the work over the long haul. Not sloppy and not slapdash. Diligence implies steady, faithful work. Painstaking means *taking pains* to do a good job.

The woman described in Proverbs 31 is nothing if not diligent, so let's examine some of the verses that describe her activities and see if we can't get a good picture of diligence to imitate.

Verse 13: "She seeks wool and flax, and willingly works with her hands." Note the verbs in this sentence: *seeks* and *works.* And notice that the adverb describing how she seeks and works is *willingly*. A willing worker is a cheerful worker. You know how an unwilling worker looks, with a long face and a grumpy attitude.

Since all our work is to be offered unto the Lord, these are the attitudes that should accompany our work: willingness and cheerfulness. The woman described here is using her hands to beautify and glorify.

For this woman, her calling is her work, and she is called to manage a large household.

Verse 15: "She also rises while it is yet night and provides food for her household and a portion for her maidservants." She is an early bird and gets a running start on the day.

Verse 17: "She girds herself with strength, and strengthens her arms." She is not a wimp; she is not afraid of work.

Verse 18: "Her lamp does not go out by night." This is a woman who does not work by the clock. She doesn't assume she's done with her work just because the sun went down.

Verse 27: "She watches over the ways of her household, and does not eat the bread of idleness." She is careful to watch over her responsibilities, not slacking off, not just getting by. She's got the needs of her charges on her radar. It sounds like she can delegate and doesn't have to be the one to do everything. But when she delegates, she makes sure that there is follow-through.

Idleness is always a danger, and this woman isn't giving way to it. You won't catch her zoned out on her computer or smartphone, spending hours on social media. She has too much to do! The Bible has a particular warning for women who are time wasters: "For of this sort are those who creep into households and make captives of gullible women loaded down with sins, led away by various lusts, always learning and never able to come to the knowledge of the truth" (2 Tim 3:6). These women are vulnerable because they have the burden of a guilty conscience and are easily led astray. They are physically lazy and intellectually lazy, so they are easy prey for false teachers.

Here's another admonition to women on the dangers of idleness:

> But refuse the younger widows; for when they have begun to grow wanton against Christ they desire to marry, having condemnation because they have cast off their first faith. And besides they learn to be *idle*, wandering about from house to house, and not only idle but also gossips and busybodies, saying things which they ought not. Therefore I desire that the younger widows marry, bear children, manage the house, give no opportunity to the adversary to speak reproachfully. For some have already turned aside after Satan. (1 Tim. 5:11–15)

God's cure for idleness in young women is marriage, children, and home management. He gives them something profoundly important to do that requires long-term diligence.

Not only does God hate laziness, but He blesses diligence.

> The lazy man does not roast what he took in hunting, But *diligence* is man's precious possession. (Prov. 12:27)
>
> He who has a slack hand becomes poor, but the hand of the *diligent* makes rich. (Prov. 10:4)
>
> The hand of the *diligent* will rule, but the lazy man will be put to forced labor. (Prov. 12:24)
>
> The soul of a lazy man desires, and has nothing; but the soul of the *diligent* shall be made rich. (Prov. 13:4)

Spiritual Diligence

All diligence must first begin with spiritual diligence. If we are spiritually lazy, we will be lazy at our work as well.

> Let us therefore be *diligent* to enter that rest, lest anyone fall according to the same example of disobedience. (Heb. 4:11)
>
> *Pursue* peace with all people, and holiness, without which no one will see the Lord, *looking carefully* lest anyone fall short of the grace of God; lest any root of bitterness springing up cause trouble, and by this many become defiled. (Heb. 12:14–15)

And beside this, *giving all diligence*, add to your faith virtue...
(2 Pet. 1:5)

God wants His people to be fruitful. Fruitfulness is Spirit-filled obedience to God's commands. All of them! We are to be hard working when it comes to our calling, and we are to give all diligence when it comes to our faith. We are to make our calling and election sure. We are to look carefully after the state of our own souls. Our Christian life is something we are to tend, which means we are paying attention, watching, and working, and all by the grace of God.

QUESTIONS

1. Consider your day from when you wake up until when you shut your eyes at night. Are there any times during the day when you are typically idle? How can you take dominion of that time and make it more fruitful?

2. How does idleness differ from relaxation and recreation?

3. Does God want His people to be workaholics? How does fruitfulness differ from busyness?

4. What is the world's idea of how much work a person should do? Is this a biblical view?

5. Which areas in our homes could use more attention from us? What hinders us from tackling those areas?

3

CHEERFULNESS

A cheerful woman is contented and happy, pleasant to be around. As we consider cheerfulness, we must remember that this is not about having a naturally cheerful disposition, but rather choosing to be a cheerful person even when we do *not* feel like it. We all like to be around cheerful people, not gloomy people. Though Eeyore is a likeable character in *Winnie the Pooh*, the author is making fun of his gloomy disposition. Tigger is the exaggerated form of the cheerful soul. We want to strike a balance so that we are neither of these extremes.

When we "cheer" for our favorite team, we are encouraging them loudly. We might say, "Cheer up!" to a friend who is glum, or describe someone who is jolly as cheerful (full of cheeriness).

The source and direction of our happiness is of course God. Some people are naturally cheerful, but to be consistently cheerful with a deep happiness, we must be happy in God. He enables us to be happy, and we glorify Him by being happy. Cheerfulness is something that should characterize our lives; we should not be cheerful from time to time, but rather consistently.

We have a duty as Christians to be cheerful. Look at the verses below. Happiness is the result of having our sins forgiven, the result of being God's children. We have no excuse! Cheerfulness is an expression of this happiness.

> Happy are the people whose God is the Lord! (Ps. 144:15b)

> Happy is he who has the God of Jacob for his help, whose hope is in the Lord his God. (Ps. 146:5)

> Then behold, they brought to Him a paralytic lying on a bed. When Jesus saw their faith, He said to the paralytic, "Son, be of good cheer; your sins are forgiven you." (Mt. 9:2)

When are we cheerful?

1. Giving

"So let each one give as he purposes in his heart, not grudgingly or of necessity; for God loves a cheerful giver" (2 Cor. 9:7).

Whether we are giving someone a ride, a drink, an encouraging word, money, or help of any kind, we should be giving gladly. God does not delight in our giving if it is done half-heartedly or with a grumpy spirit. When we purpose to do so cheerfully, we receive a blessing from God.

2. Singing

"Is anyone cheerful? Let him sing psalms" (Jas. 5:13b). Singing is an outlet for our happiness, whether it is at church, at home, in the car, at school, or in the shower!

3. Showing Mercy

"He who shows mercy, with cheerfulness" (Rom. 12:8b). Showing mercy is being considerate toward others whether they are children, the elderly, the stranger, the lonely, or the sales clerk.

Proverbs 14:21 says, "He who despises his neighbor sins; but he who has mercy on the poor, happy is he." Good deeds of all kinds are acts of mercy. The result of such good works is happiness. God bestows a blessing on us when we are kind to others.

4. Fearing the Lord and Walking with Him

"Blessed [or happy] is every one who fears the Lord, who walks in His ways" (Ps. 128:1). This means that we are not to fear our enemies, but rather we should fear God who delivers us.

Thomas Watson, the great Puritan preacher, said, "Faith keeps the heart cheerful, fear keeps the heart serious." We are to walk uprightly before the Lord, and we will be happy people. To fear the Lord is to worship Him. The Lord's Supper strengthens, revives us, and renews us. Communion with the saints blesses us and refreshes us. We are to continue steadfastly in prayer (Rom. 12:12). When discussing prayer, Watson said, "It is a key that unlocks the treasury of God's mercy. Prayer keeps the heart open to God and shut to sin."

5. Working and Eating

"When you eat the labor of your hands, you shall be happy, and it shall be well with you" (Ps. 128:2). When we walk in the fear of the Lord, all we do is done unto Him. Eating the fruit of our labor is describing the benefit we receive from our own honest labor. So as we sit down and serve the pie we made, we are enjoying the fruit of our labor, and this makes us cheerful and thankful.

We are to serve the Lord "not lagging in diligence, fervent in spirit" (Rom. 12:11). As we work hard before the Lord, we are blessed with happiness in Him. We are satisfied.

6. Showing Hospitality

We are to "be hospitable to one another without grumbling" (1 Pet. 4:9). Hospitality is about friendliness and welcoming people into your home with open hearts. A grumpy attitude is antithetical to true hospitality. Open hearts throw open the doors cheerfully. A grumbling heart cannot show genuine hospitality. We should never complain about having people over! Nor should we discourage others when they are being hospitable. This can sometimes be motivated by compassion, but it might be more of a stumbling block than we realize. "You're having company again? Don't you get tired of it?"

7. Finding Wisdom

"Happy is the man who finds wisdom and the man who gains understanding" (Prov. 3:13). We find wisdom when we seek it diligently. That means we pay attention to the Word preached; we seek instruction, guidance, and counsel from God's Word. If we want to be happy people, we must take the pursuit of wisdom seriously, and God promises that we will be happy when we find it.

8. Heeding the Word and Trusting the Lord

"He who heeds the word wisely will find good, and whoever trusts in the Lord, happy is he" (Prov. 16:20). This means that not only do we hear and learn wisdom, we do it. This is very important because just hearing the Word is not enough. We want to be doers not just hearers (Jas. 1:22). So when you learn something, apply it. Otherwise you will lose the ground you have gained. Notice that we are happy when we trust the Lord. When we drift away and become worrisome or self-absorbed, we lose our joy.

9. Keeping the law

"Where there is no revelation, the people cast off restraint; but happy is he who keeps the law" (Prov. 29:18). What a blessing it is to have God's law written on our hearts and to have a regenerated heart that wants to obey God. When we obey Him, we are happy. It sounds very simple, because it is simple. Sometimes it is hard to obey, but it is never impossible. God has promised to give us His Spirit, and by the means of the Spirit, we are enabled to do what is right.

Hindrances

So what is it that hinders cheerfulness? We all like cheerfulness, and we like being cheerful, so why aren't we simply cheerful all the time? Sin is always the culprit. Here are four broad headings of sin that keep us from being cheerful people.

1. Unbelief

Unbelief is forgetfulness. We forget who we are in Christ; we forget how glorious and powerful our God is. We forget His promises to us, and all this causes us to lose heart.

2. Impatience

We become full of ourselves and forget how patient God has been with us. We want instant sanctification (for ourselves or others) or instant answers to our prayers. God is working His will in the world. We must not lose sight of His sovereign control over all things.

3. Ingratitude

When we fail to be thankful to God for all things, we quickly forget how much God has done in and for us. We think more highly of ourselves than we ought and think we "deserve" better treatment.

4. Bitterness

When we keep a record of other people's wrongs against us, we lose our joy (Heb. 12:15). When bitterness fills our minds and hearts, we can't think of anything but how we have been wronged. It's a sad state to be in.

These ugly attitudes often manifest themselves in murmuring, complaining, grumbling, self-pity, and other forms of discontent. This is unworthy of a Christian. Philippians 2:14 says, "Do all things without complaining or disputing." Remember that murmuring not only fails to make things better, it makes things worse.

The Effects of Grumbling

1. Grumbling is a bad example and can cause others to join you in the same sin.
2. Grumbling distracts you away from the duties that God has given you to do.
3. Grumbling often leads to other sins like self-pity, worry, annoyance, and disrespect.
4. Hearing yourself complain just reinforces your bad attitude and makes things seem even worse than they are.
5. Complaining is not only unproductive (nothing good comes of it), but it is destructive. It tears people down.
6. Complaining is just a big waste of time. You could be doing something worthwhile.
7. God hates grumbling and complaining, and He will judge it! Think of the Israelites in the wilderness.

QUESTIONS

1. How can we be cheerful when we don't feel like it?

2. How do we stay cheerful and happy in the midst of a trial?

3. What is the hardest thing for you to be cheerful about?

4. How can we correct the bad habit of mumbling and complaining?

5. If we find ourselves doing outwardly good things (like showing hospitality) with an inwardly grudging spirit, how can we correct it?

4
CONTENTMENT

Contentment is a very useful virtue to learn and apply, because with contentment we can be comfortable in all kinds of situations. In fact, when we get good at it, we can be comfortable in every situation. My mother-in-law defined Christian contentment as a deep satisfaction with the will of God. If we know that God works all things for our good and His glory, then we can accept our circumstances with contentment.

If we have easy circumstances, then it's fairly easy to assume we are content. But difficult circumstances show us who we really are. In those cases it is far easier to be dissatisfied and discontent, disappointed and discouraged. Notice that Paul says that he has learned to be content in all kinds of circumstances, not just in the easy ones. He says he can be content *everywhere* and in *everything*.

> Not that I speak in regard to need, for I have learned in whatever state I am, to be content: I know how to be abased, and I know how to abound. Everywhere and in all things I have learned both to be full and to be hungry, both to abound and to suffer need. I can do all things through Christ who strengthens me. (Phil. 4:11–13)

Contentment is a close cousin to cheerfulness, because, really, you can't have a cheerful spirit if you are discontent. Many of the virtues are like this: they all grow on the same tree. So if you are increasing in virtue in one area, then you can expect that you will be growing in others. If you are growing in cheerfulness, you will be growing in contentment.

The Source of Our Contentment

Notice that the passage in Philippians above includes the famous verse "I can do all things through Christ who strengthens me." We often see this verse quoted in many contexts, but seldom do we see it connected to the prior verses. The *all things* he refers to is being content in all circumstances. In other words, contentment is through the strength of Christ and not at all through our own strength.

Jesus freely gives us Himself and enables us to do something that is beyond our own strength.

We Learn Contentment

If the apostle Paul had to learn this virtue, then it is not something that we can expect to do naturally on our own. We have to learn it as well. And judging from Paul's life, he had plenty of opportunities to learn. Look at 2 Corinthians 11:23–27:

> Are they ministers of Christ?—I speak as a fool—I am more: in labors more abundant, in stripes above measure, in prisons more frequently, in deaths often. From the Jews five times I received forty stripes minus one. Three times I was beaten with rods; once I was stoned; three times I was shipwrecked; a night and a day I have been in the deep; in journeys often, in perils of waters, in perils of robbers, in perils of my own countrymen, in perils of the Gentiles, in perils in the city, in perils in the wilderness, in perils in the sea, in perils among false brethren; in weariness and toil, in sleeplessness often, in hunger and thirst, in fastings often, in cold and nakedness

Contentment in Hard Circumstances

Paul had some very challenging circumstances:

- He was whipped many times.
- He was in prison many times.
- He nearly died several times.
- Five times the Jews whipped him with 39 lashes.
- He was beaten with rods on three occasions.
- He was stoned once.
- He was shipwrecked three times and spent a night and a day in the sea.
- He was often in danger.
- He was in danger from false brothers.
- He suffered weariness, painfulness, sleeplessness.
- He was often hungry and thirsty and without food or drink.
- He was often cold and naked.

I think this should be enough to qualify Paul to speak to us about contentment. But remember, the only way he found contentment was through the strength of Christ, not his own ability. When he was in jail after being beaten (Acts 16:25), he and Silas were "praying and singing hymns to God." That is when God sent an earthquake and broke open the prison doors.

The focus of contentment is Christ. The focus of discontent is the trouble. Paul and Silas were focusing on God in the midst of their trouble. That's what we want to learn to do.

Two Sources of Discontent

The signs of discontent are grumbling, envy, anger, and complaining (to name a few). Discontent is a restless desire for something else or something more. It goes hand-in-hand with envy: when we see the blessings others have, we fail to see our own blessings, and we want theirs.

We can narrow this down to two basic areas of life where we are tempted to be discontent.

1. Things We Have

"Let your conduct be without covetousness; be content with such things as you have. For He Himself has said, 'I will never leave you nor forsake you'" (Heb. 13:5). When we are discontent, we look at what we have and there is something wrong with it. It isn't enough or it isn't right or it isn't the best. But whatever our circumstances or possessions, God has given us something very precious: Jesus has promised that He will never leave or forsake His people. No matter how difficult things might be, you can know that Jesus is with you. That is by far the best reason for contentment. No matter how difficult it might be, our Savior is with us and will strengthen us.

2. Things We Don't Have

Jesus said, "Take heed and beware of covetousness, for one's life does not consist in the abundance of the things he possesses" (Lk. 12:15). We sometimes think that if we could just add the things that are missing to our life, then we would be content. But the sad truth is that no matter how much stuff we get, we can always think of something else we want. For example, a discontented single woman will take her discontent with her into marriage. A change in circumstances won't bring contentment to a discontented soul. So we have to find out how to be content.

A Few Steps to Take to Learn Contentment

1. Express appreciation to God for your blessings and for His promises to you. Choose to be thankful whether you "feel" like it or not. Tell God you want to be satisfied with all He is doing in your life.
2. Confess any covetousness. Contentment can't live alongside covetousness, because the covetousness will crowd out contentment and fuel envy. We see what

someone else has, and we notice that we don't have it. And we want it. That is covetousness. When we covet, we are breaking one of God's commandments.

3. Remember that all things truly do work together for good to those who love God and are called according to His purpose (Rom. 8:28). God ordains all things that come to pass. He is a wise and loving Father. He will use all these things for our good—so interpret the situation in a way that sees God as doing that right now.
4. Ask yourself, "What are my duties in this situation?" Does God want you to mope and feel sorry for yourself? Your mind-set should be on how to glorify Him and turn a profit on this difficulty. What can I learn from this? How can I be a good steward of this difficulty? How can I please God in it? This helps us see the difficulty not as something God is doing *to* us but rather as what He is doing *for* us.
5. What is the opposite of contentment? Murmuring and complaining. Pay attention to your thoughts and words. Do you sound content? In many cases, the discontent is worse than the circumstances! By being content, we sweeten even the worst of situations, while discontent only makes them worse. So contentment may not

change our hard circumstances, but it will make the situation more comfortable for us to bear.

6. Be humble. Rather than thinking you deserve better, be grateful for what you have. Learn to put others first.
7. Keep a clear conscience before God. Sin always muddies the water so you can't see clearly.

To Sum Up

1. Contentment is sweet. It makes all situations better, while discontent makes them worse.
2. Contentment keeps us from many other sins like covetousness, envy, anger, murmuring, or an ungodly competition with others.
3. Our possessions will never satisfy our souls. Only Christ can satisfy us and bring us the deep satisfaction we all hunger for.
4. Contentment gives us victory over ourselves. Remember Christians are to take up their cross and die to themselves.
5. When we choose to be cheerful and thankful, our spirits are quieted and we can rest in God.

ASSIGNMENT

Make a list of your discontents. Make one column for things you have that you are discontent about and a second column for things you don't have. Then pray through this list, confessing the discontent and thanking God for what He is doing in your life. Pray that you will learn contentment in each of these things.

My sources for this chapter include two great Puritan books: *The Rare Jewel of Christian Contentment* by Jeremiah Burroughs and *The Art of Divine Contentment* by Thomas Watson.

5

PRUDENCE

Some of these virtues are characteristics we recognize and appreciate, but others are not really familiar territory. Take prudence for an example. How often do you hear someone use that term or name their daughter Prudence? But it was a popular Puritan name, and in a word, *prudence* means *caution.* Prudence is obviously a big deal to God because just look at this verse below: "Houses and riches are an inheritance from fathers, but a prudent wife is from the Lord" (Prov. 19:14).

It's clear that this prudent woman is a prize. She is set over against houses, riches, and an inheritance, which are the best things a father can give his son. But God can do better. He can give a prudent wife. Given that the Lord thinks a prudent wife is such a prize, we should give this virtue our attention and find out what prudence entails. Closely related to the term *prudence* is *discretion,* and each is often used in defining the other.

God doesn't think much of a woman without discretion. Take a look at this: "As a ring of gold in a swine's snout, so is a lovely woman who lacks discretion" (Prov. 11:22). I can't think of anything much more ridiculous than a pig wearing jewelry. That's what an indiscreet, but beautiful, woman is compared to. So all the more reason for us to search out what prudence and discretion are and how we can adorn ourselves appropriately with them.

Prudence and discretion are often mentioned together in the same verse, as in Proverbs 8:12: "I, wisdom, dwell with prudence, and find out knowledge and discretion." We see here that both prudence and discretion keep company with wisdom and knowledge. And notice that wisdom is *searching out* discretion. Our lives should be characterized by a desire for more; not more stuff, but more knowledge and wisdom. When we seek first the kingdom of God and His righteousness, He will take care of food and clothing and all we need (Mt. 6:33). Part of seeking His righteousness is to be diligently adding virtue to our faith and searching for more wisdom and more spiritual knowledge. Think of wisdom and prudence as scholarly companions reading fat books full of godly knowledge and wisdom. That's what a prudent wife is like.

Let's look at more characteristics of discretion and prudence.

"The discretion of a man makes him slow to anger, and his glory is to overlook a transgression" (Prov. 19:11). If we have discretion, we are safeguarded against quick or angry reactions. We will act, and not react. The fruit of discretion is patience and forgiveness, so there is no keeping a record of wrongs. This in itself is a glory-bestowing trait.

"The simple believes every word, but the prudent considers well his steps" (Prov. 14:15). Prudence is not gullible (like the idle women in 2 Tim. 3:6). She is a little cynical and cautious about what she hears, and she's slow to pass on tales. Not only that, but she is far-sighted and can anticipate what the consequences of her behavior might be. That's why she carefully considers her next step, and she doesn't lurch. She thinks things over and takes her time. She is not impulsive or driven by her emotions.

"The wise in heart will be called prudent, and sweetness of the lips increases learning" (Proverbs 16:21). Prudence begins in the heart of a wise woman, and like everything else in our hearts, it comes out her mouth. Jesus said, "For out of the abundance of the heart his mouth speaks" (Luke

6:45). In the case of the prudent, it comes out in sweetness. Also notice that this sweetness increases learning. It is edifying and builds up—not at all like the foolish woman in Proverbs 14:1 who is pulling down her house with her own hands.

"The heart of the prudent acquires knowledge, and the ear of the wise seeks knowledge" (Proverbs 18:15). We see again this theme of seriously pursuing knowledge and wisdom. Prudence is a heart attitude, not an IQ level. It is not lazy, but is studying God's Word for more knowledge. I hope you have noticed how often these virtues are connected with knowledge and learning. A wise woman is acquiring knowledge, seeking knowledge, and increasing in learning. She is not intellectually lazy.

"When wisdom enters your heart, and knowledge is pleasant to your soul, discretion will preserve you; understanding will keep you, to deliver you from the way of evil, from the man who speaks perverse things" (Proverbs 2:10–12). For those who are like Prudence and Discretion, wisdom and knowledge are pleasant. And notice the benefits of discretion: it preserves, keeps, and delivers.

A lack of discretion, on the other hand, is often associated with the tongue. And take special note here: a discreet woman is wise enough to steer clear of perverse men. You know what kind I mean: the ones who have exchanged good for evil and call evil good. Keep your distance from those guys.

And one last thing before we finish. One of the other godly traits mentioned in Scripture is discernment. This is the ability to see clearly and have good sense. Discernment knows how to make distinctions between right and wrong and shows good judgment. It is a sign of maturity and experience. It takes practice. Those who are prudent and discreet have discernment because they have been trained by God's Word. Let's look briefly at a few more verses that mention discernment.

> But solid food belongs to those who are of full age, that is, those who by reason of use have their senses exercised to discern both good and evil. (Heb. 5:14)

> But the natural man does not receive the things of the Spirit of God, for they are foolishness to him; nor can he know them, because they are spiritually discerned. (1 Cor. 2:14)

> For the word of God is living and powerful, and sharper than any two-edged sword, piercing even to the division of soul and spirit, and of joints and marrow, and is a discerner of the thoughts and intents of the heart. (Heb. 4:12)

So you see here that only the wise Christian has spiritual discernment. Not until God opens our eyes can we see. And once our eyes are open, we can discern spiritual things. In other words, then the Bible makes sense. The Bible is the ultimate source of all these virtues we have been discussing. If we are not studying His Word, we can't expect to gain wisdom, knowledge, prudence, discretion, or discernment. The more familiar we are with the Bible, the more discernment we gain.

QUESTIONS

1. How are prudence and discretion related? What do they have in common?

2. Why does prudence make a wife a real prize?

3. In what ways do you need to apply prudence and discretion, particularly in your relationships or friendships with men?

4. How can discretion protect you?

5. How can discernment help us understand the times we live in?

6

WISDOM

Wisdom is personified as a woman in the book of Proverbs, so any treatment of feminine virtues must have wisdom at its foundation. In fact, Proverbs 4:7 tells us that "Wisdom is the principal thing; Therefore get wisdom. And in all your getting, get understanding." Wisdom is not really optional for the Christian. We are to make it the most important thing. If we are seeking to glorify God in all we do, then we are pursuing wisdom. Foolishness never glorifies God, and wisdom always does.

Wisdom is the ability to judge correctly and make God-honoring decisions. Wisdom comes from obeying God and following His Word closely. We grow in wisdom as we experience His faithfulness, and we grow in wisdom as we trust Him for the future. We please God when we walk in wisdom, and we please God when we ask Him for wisdom. "If any of you lacks wisdom, let him ask of God, who gives to all liberally and without reproach, and it will be given to him" (Jas. 1:5).

Solomon was the wisest man in the world, so Proverbs is the map to find the gold mine that is wisdom.

All wisdom comes from God. He created the world by His wisdom.

> There is no wisdom or understanding or counsel against the Lord. (Prov. 21:30)

> The fear of the Lord is the beginning of wisdom, and the knowledge of the Holy One is understanding. For by me your days will be multiplied and years of life will be added to you. (Prov. 9:10–11)

> The Lord by wisdom founded the earth; by understanding He established the heavens; by His knowledge the depths were broken up, and clouds drop down the dew. (Prov. 3:19–20)

WE MUST SEARCH FOR WISDOM LIKE WE WOULD SEARCH FOR TREASURE.

> Happy is the man who finds wisdom, and the man who gains understanding. (Prov. 3:13)

> Get wisdom! Get understanding! Do not forget, nor turn away from the words of my mouth. (Prov. 4:5)

And Wisdom says, "Those who seek me diligently will find me" (Prov. 8:17b). No matter how old we are, we should still seek wisdom diligently. The Christian life is a journey. We are to be pressing on, not coasting. In fact, when we settle in to coasting, we find that we are actually going backwards.

WISDOM IS WEALTH AND HONOR.

> Exalt her, and she will promote you; she will bring you honor, when you embrace her. She will place on your head an ornament of grace; a crown of glory she will deliver to you. (Prov. 4:8–9)

> For her proceeds are better than the profits of silver, and her gain than fine gold. She is more precious than rubies and all the things you may desire cannot compare with her. Length of days is in her right hand, in her left hand riches and honor. (Prov. 3:14–16)

> For wisdom is better than rubies, and all the things one may desire cannot be compared with her. I, wisdom, dwell with prudence, and find out knowledge and discretion. (Prov. 8:11–12)

> How much better to get wisdom than gold! And to get understanding is to be chosen rather than silver. (Prov. 16:16)

A wise woman is honorable, full of grace, glorious, and of great worth. She has a precious possession (wisdom) that cannot be taken from her. Think of a beautiful jewelry box full of rare jewels. You would treasure it and keep it safe. That is what wisdom is like.

We are to wear it on our head (like a crown), which means our wisdom is visible. We are to use it (in our right hand and in our left). We are never to be without wisdom.

WISDOM IS GOOD, PLEASANT, AND PEACEFUL, A SOURCE OF HAPPINESS.

> Her [Wisdom's] ways are ways of pleasantness, and all her paths are peace. She is a tree of life to those who take hold of her, and happy are all who retain her. (Prov. 3:17–18)

> He who gets wisdom loves his own soul; He who keeps understanding will find good. (Prov. 19:8)

A wise woman has a deep happiness and peace that is spiritual, not worldly. Her life is fruitful, and her soul is healthy and prospering. She is not fretful or restless or worried.

Wisdom is a protection for those who hang on to her.

> My son, let them not depart from your eyes—keep sound wisdom and discretion; so they will be life to your soul and grace to your neck. Then you will walk safely in your way and your foot will not stumble. (Prov. 3:21–23)

> Do not forsake her [Wisdom], and she will preserve you; love her, and she will keep you. (Prov. 4:6)

We all know people who have gotten into troubles and tangles by their own foolish behavior and choices. But wisdom keeps us from doing stupid things. Wisdom is not trying to please the crowd, but wants to please God. The foolish trouble their own souls while the wise have a clean conscience.

Wisdom listens to and obeys counsel and instruction.

> The way of a fool is right in his own eyes, but he who heeds counsel is wise. (Prov. 12:15)

> A wise son heeds his father's instruction, but a scoffer does not listen to rebuke. (Prov. 13:1)

> Give instruction to a wise man, and he will be still wiser; teach a just man, and he will increase in learning. (Prov. 9:9)

Wisdom is humble. It will listen to advice, especially when it comes from parents. The wise woman doesn't think she is always right. She is willing to take correction and doesn't bristle. She hunts for wisdom in God's Word and weighs the advice she is given against God's Word.

WISDOM IS STRENGTH.

The more we believe God, the more our faith grows and the stronger it gets.

> "A wise man is strong, Yes, a man of knowledge increases strength" (Prov. 24:5).

A wise woman looks to God to strengthen her faith, like Abraham did:

> And not being weak in faith, he did not consider his own body, already dead (since he was about a hundred years old), and the deadness of Sarah's womb. He did not waver at the promise of God through unbelief, but was strengthened in faith, giving

> glory to God, and being fully convinced that what He had promised He was also able to perform. (Rom. 4:19–21)

Wisdom doesn't give emotions the steering wheel.

> A fool vents all his feelings, but a wise man holds them back. (Prov. 29:11)

> Whoever has no rule over his own spirit is like a city broken down, without walls. (Prov. 25:28)

It is easy to let your emotions tell you what to do, but a wise woman stays in control, keeping her emotions out of the driver's seat. When we have no control over our own spirit, we are giving the enemy free access to our heart and mind. Wisdom has rule over her own spirit. She does not have a bad day because she feels a little blue. She chooses to ignore her feelings and do the right thing in all circumstances. She looks for her duties today in her current situation. She is particularly careful about saying too much (venting).

Foolishness, on the other hand . . .

The opposite of wisdom is foolishness. All sin is foolishness, and all foolishness is sin. Proverbs has quite a bit to say about fools: Wisdom is constructive; foolishness is destructive, simple (stupid), and mouthy. But let's look at some particular references to foolish women.

"The wise woman builds her house, but the foolish pulls it down with her hands" (Prov. 14:1). The wise woman has a particular calling to make her home a place where wisdom reigns. The foolish woman is tearing up her house, often with her own mouth or hands, criticizing and complaining and being lazy and destructive. It's no surprise when she finds her home in heaps around her feet.

"A foolish woman is clamorous; she is simple, and knows nothing" (Prov. 9:13). While a wise woman weighs her words, the foolish woman is blabbing and noisy. She makes a hubbub where ever she goes. She displays her ignorance and lack of wisdom by her words and behavior.

Job's wife was foolish when she told her husband to curse God and die. In his famous response, he says, "You speak as one of the foolish women speaks" (Job 2:10a). The world has never lacked for foolish women. The wise woman provides a stark contrast.

QUESTIONS

1. How do we pursue wisdom?

2. What might hinder us from pursuing wisdom?

3. What are some of the qualities of the wise woman?

4. How does wisdom protect us?

5. How does a wise woman control her emotions?

6. How does wisdom relate to the tongue?

7

HUMILITY

No list of Christian virtues can be complete without humility. This is a central part of the gospel, so it is central to the Christian life. Jesus humbled himself to the point of death on a cross, and we are told in Paul's letter to Philippians to "let this mind be in you which was also in Christ Jesus" (Phil. 2:5). We follow our humble Savior when we humble ourselves.

> And being found in appearance as a man, He humbled Himself and became obedient to the point of death, even the death of the cross. Therefore God also has highly exalted Him and given Him the name which is above every name, that at the name of Jesus every knee should bow, of those in heaven, and of those on earth, and of those under the earth, and that every tongue

should confess that Jesus Christ is Lord, to the glory of God the Father. (Phil. 2:8–11)

A Humble Mind-set

Jesus laid down the privileges of His status as the Son of God, He humbled Himself and became a man so that He could die for His church. He obeyed God, even going to a shameful death on a cross for us. This is our model for humility.

But humility is not our natural tendency. Rather, we naturally tend to exalt ourselves, to think of ourselves as better or more important than others, and to look out for ourselves. Humility is not easy. We exaggerate our own importance, and we see the defects and shortcomings of others. Basically, pride is the enemy of humility. But we are called to humility, and we are to seek it and find it. Where do we look for humility? We look to the author of humility, God Himself. "Seek the Lord, all you meek of the earth, who have upheld His justice. Seek righteousness, seek *humility*" (Zeph. 2:3).

Humble is a verb.

Jesus told us the way up is down. "For whoever exalts himself will be humbled, and he who *humbles* himself will be exalted" (Lk. 14:11). So it is better to humble ourselves than to be humbled by God. When we are humbled by someone else, it is humiliating. We are not called to humble others; we are called to humble ourselves.

> Therefore whoever *humbles* himself as this little child is the greatest in the kingdom of heaven. (Mt. 18:4)

> Therefore *humble* yourselves under the mighty hand of God, that He may exalt you in due time. (1 Pet. 5:6a)

> *Humble* yourselves in the sight of the Lord, and He will lift you up. (James 4:10)

> But He gives more grace. Therefore He says, 'God resists the proud, but gives grace to the *humble*. (Jas. 4:6)

God loves the humble in spirit. He exalts, lifts up, and gives more grace to the humble-hearted. So we should want to get a humble spirit! But how do we get a humble spirit? I already mentioned that it's not easy, and it's not natural. But we must be able to do it because we are commanded to humble ourselves.

To humble yourself is to get under God's feet. You acknowledge that He is Lord and you are not. You confess your sins and thank Him for His forgiveness. You submit to His authority over you. This is humility before God.

God blesses the humble.

> The humble He guides in justice, and the humble He teaches His way. (Ps. 25:9)

> By humility and the fear of the Lord are riches and honor and life. (Prov. 22:4)

> The Lord lifts up the humble; He casts the wicked down to the ground. (Ps. 147:6)

If we want to experience God's blessing, we must be a humble people. He will guide us and teach us, He will bless us with life, honor, and riches, and He will lift us up. The humble are in the position (a lowly position) to receive great good from their loving God.

But how are we to be humble toward others?

"Be of the same mind toward one another. Do not set your mind of high things, but associate with the *humble*. Do not be wise in your own opinion" (Rom. 12:16). Humility is willing to get along with others (having the same mind). It isn't trying to show off or display its own talents and abilities, but chooses lowly people (humble people) for its friends. And humility never sees itself as wise. The odd thing is that wise people see how far they still have to go.

The foolish think they are wise already. "Remind them to be subject to rulers and authorities, to obey, to be ready for every good work, to speak evil of no one, to be peaceable, gentle, showing all *humility* to all men" (Tit. 3:1–2).

1. Humility has a high view of God and a low view of itself.
2. Humility is obedient. This means a student obeys her teacher, a daughter obeys her parents, a wife obeys her husband, a worker obeys her boss, a church member obeys the elders, a citizen obeys the speed limit and pays her taxes.
3. The humble are eager for good works, and if you think about this, most good works benefit others. I am to be eager to help others, because I am already eager to help myself.
4. Humility has a wise and tender-hearted tongue, so it doesn't bad-mouth others.
5. Humility is not argumentative for the sake of arguing. It is eager to get along with others.
6. Humility is gentle and courteous. She is compassionate and kindly.
7. Humility listens and is teachable.

8. Humility seeks forgiveness for sin and puts things right with others.
9. Humility gives way to others, serving others first, giving others the best seat or the biggest piece of pie.
10. Finally, humility is to be exhibited toward everyone, not just to those in authority over us.

God hates pride.

The opposite of humility is *pride.* This is most easily identified as feeling overly pleased with ourselves.

Pride is a blinding and hardening sin. The more we indulge it, the worse it gets.

> These six things the Lord hates, Yes, seven are an abomination to Him: a proud look . . . (Prov. 6:16–17a)

> Pride goes before destruction, and a haughty spirit before a fall. Better to be of a humble spirit with the lowly, than to divide the spoil with the proud. (Prov. 16:18–19)

> Whoever secretly slanders his neighbor, Him I will destroy; the one who has a haughty look and a proud heart, Him I will not endure. (Ps. 101: 5)

> He who is of a proud heart stirs up strife, but he who trusts in the Lord will be prospered. (Prov. 28:25)

God hates pride, and pride is the herald for destruction and a fall. We should hate pride every time we see it in ourselves.

How do we know if we are proud?

1. The proud slander others, passing on lies.
2. The proud look down on others, considering themselves to be better.
3. The proud love to stir up trouble, causing quarrels.
4. The proud react to pride in others. ("Who does she think she is?")
5. A proud spirit does not receive correction.
6. A proud spirit does not take trouble for others.

Finally, the humble love to hear God's praises.

"I will bless the Lord at all times; His praise shall continually be in my mouth; my soul shall make its boast in the Lord; the humble shall hear of it and be glad" (Ps. 34:1–2). The humble gather to worship God and rejoice to praise Him.

QUESTIONS

1. How does Christ set the standard for humility?

2. Why does our flesh have such a hard time being humble?

3. Why does God love the humble?

4. What is the benefit of humility?

5. How can we identify pride in ourselves?

8

COURAGE

Courage is not something people necessarily think of as a feminine virtue, but I think there are good grounds to believe otherwise. Courage is a virtue that enables us to be fearless and brave in painful, difficult, or dangerous situations. A courageous woman can be described as plucky (there's a word you don't hear often).

Remember that the word "virtue" comes from the Latin word that means manliness or manly courage. So to be virtuous women, we must forsake cowardliness and embrace a biblical femininity. Proverbs 12:4a says, "An excellent wife is the crown of her husband." As noted earlier, the *New Geneva Study Bible* says this literally means "a wife of valor." Now I like that: Christian women are to have a backbone if they want to be a crown to their husbands. A wife who is cowardly will not be an *excellent* wife. Sometimes we mistakenly think that a weak, frail, whimpering wife is what a strong, godly man wants in order to show off his manly strength. But the truth is that kind of woman ends up being more of a liability than a blessing. We are to be courageous women, and we have many biblical examples to follow of women with true faith and courage.

The command to be brave

Take a look at this sampling of Scriptures that address all Christians to be courageous. It is not just the men who need to be brave, but all believers. To "stand fast" is to hold your ground and not yield.

> Watch, *stand fast* in the faith, be *brave*, be *strong*. (1 Cor. 16:13)
>
> Only let your conduct be worthy of the gospel of Christ, so that whether I come and see you or am absent, I may hear of your affairs, that you *stand fast* in one spirit, with one mind striving together for the faith of the gospel, and *not* in any way *terrified* by your adversaries, which is to them a proof of perdition, but to you of salvation, and that from God. (Phil. 1:27–28)
>
> Therefore, my beloved and longed-for brethren, my joy and crown, so *stand fast* in the Lord, beloved. (Phil. 4:1)

THE SOURCE OF OUR COURAGE IS GOD.

Of course, like all virtues, God is our example, and He is the One who gives us strength by means of His power and might to obey all His commands, including the command to stand fast and be brave. Consider these few references below:

> I can do all things through Christ who strengthens me. (Phil. 4:13)

> . . .that He would grant you according to the riches of His glory, to be strengthened with might through His Spirit in the inner man. (Eph. 3:16)

> Finally, my brethren, be strong in the Lord and in the power of His might. (Eph. 6:10)

> Be strong and of good courage, do not fear nor be afraid of them; for the Lord your God, He is the One who goes with you. He will not leave you nor forsake you. (Deut. 31:6)

> Therefore, strengthen the hands which hang down, and the feeble knees. (Heb. 12:12)

> Wait on the Lord; be of good courage, and He shall strengthen your heart; wait, I say, on the Lord! (Ps. 27:14)

In all these verses, we see that God gives us courage. This should be a great comfort, because we may not be naturally courageous, and if it depended on us, we would be cowardly and weak. God goes with us. He will never leave us. We can believe these promises absolutely. And so you see, courage cannot operate apart from real faith in God.

We are strengthened by other saints.

Our courage and faith are gifts from God, but we can also be strengthened to be courageous by the other means God has appointed: the preaching of the Word and the fellowship of the saints.

> And when they had preached the gospel to that city and made many disciples, they returned to Lystra, Iconium, and Antioch, strengthening the souls of the disciples, exhorting them to continue in the faith, and saying, "We must through many tribulations enter the kingdom of God." (Acts 14:21–22)

> When Paul saw them, he thanked God and took courage. (Acts 28:15b)

Reading the lives of saints who laid their lives down for the gospel is another way to be strengthened and encouraged. Many faithful women have gone ahead of us, so we are in good company.

Courage and faith go together.

"[Abraham] did not waver at the promise of God through unbelief, but was strengthened in faith, giving glory to God, and being fully convinced that what He had promised He was also able to perform" (Rom. 4:20–21). It is important for us to remember that last bit: "What He had promised He was also able to perform." God never backs out of His promises, and He never fails. We must be fully convinced of this, just like Abraham was, if we want to walk in courage and faith.

And God receives all the glory. We don't pat ourselves on the back for being courageous. When we are strengthened in faith, we give the glory to God. This is not the superman version of Christianity; this is basic Christianity. We are to take God at His promises, and this will give us courage.

When do we need courage?

1. We need courage when we are afraid, when we are sick, when someone we love is sick, when we are alone.
2. We need courage when we are called to do things we have never done before, like getting married, having a baby, taking a new job, moving away from home.
3. We need courage when we have to defend the faith to scoffers, unbelievers, family members, or coworkers.

4. We will certainly need courage when we die. Thomas Watson said if we live well, we will die well. If we have exercised courage all our lives, then we will have courage at the last.

Women have a fleshly tendency to give way to fear and anxiety, and women can tag their fears as unconquerable phobias instead of having courage and doing battle with them. We need to reflect on what kinds of things we have accepted as weaknesses, and then ask God to help us to have the courage to tackle them head on.

Sarah's Daughters

> For in this manner, in former times, the holy women who trusted in God also adorned themselves, being submissive to their own husbands, as Sarah obeyed Abraham, calling him lord, whose daughters you are if you do good and are not afraid with any terror. (1 Pet. 3:5–6)

We can't prevent fears of all kinds from coming and banging on our door. But we can get the grace, strength, faith, and courage to not let those fears come into our hearts and minds. The "holy women" described above were known for their "gentle and quiet spirit, which is very precious in the sight of God" (1 Pet. 3:4). A gentle and quiet spirit is a good defensive weapon against fear. It is a spirit that is trusting God and resting in Him. It is not all churned up like white caps on a lake. When we trust God, we are able to "cast out fear" (1 Jn. 4:18). If we allow fear to come in, it requires a great deal of strength to "cast it out"! But we can. Especially if we pray for courage.

QUESTIONS

1. What are some areas where you could grow in boldness and courage?

2. Have you allowed yourself any areas of weakness? What can you do to overcome these things?

3. Do you give way to peer pressure?

4. List your fears and pray through the list, asking God to give you boldness to overcome your fears. Confess those times you have not stood fast, and thank God for His forgiveness. Now look for opportunities to be bold in Him.

9
KINDNESS

Our word "kindness" comes from the Anglo-Saxon word *cynn* which is where we get "kin" and "kinfolk" and "kinship." So, to be kind is to treat someone like family. Certainly in Christ we are all brothers and sisters, so it follows that we treat our fellow Christians like family. But that's not always easy!

To be kind is to be sympathetic, friendly, gentle, tender-hearted, generous, courteous, and affectionate (*Webster's New World College Dictionary*). That might be easier to do with those people whom you love already, but it's quite a tall order when you are called to be kind to those who are not kind in return.

As in all the virtues, God is our central example and the ultimate source of all kindness. This is His nature. His kindness even extends to His enemies.

GOD IS KIND.

> And they refused to obey, and they were not mindful of Your wonders that You did among them. But they hardened their necks and in their rebellion they appointed a leader to return to their bondage. But You are God, ready to pardon, gracious and merciful, slow to anger, *abundant in kindness,* and did not forsake them. (Neh. 9:17)

> Blessed be the Lord, for He has shown me *His marvelous kindness* in a strong city! (Ps. 31:21)

> Praise the Lord, all you Gentiles! Laud Him, all you peoples! For His *merciful kindness* is *great* toward us. And the truth of the Lord endures forever. Praise the Lord! (Ps. 117)

Notice the characteristics of God's kindness: it is abundant (plentiful); it is marvelous (astonishing); it is merciful; and it is great. It is slow to anger. It pardons. It extends even to those who do not appreciate it or understand it or who even may hate it. And to hate God's kindness is to hate Him.

We are the recipients of God's loving kindness, for "while we were still sinners, Christ died for us" (Rom. 5:8). His love has transformed us and made us into the sort of people who can extend kindness.

God is kind even to His enemies.

> But love your enemies, do good, and lend, hoping for nothing in return; and your reward will be great, and you will be sons of the Most High. For *He is kind* to the unthankful and evil. Therefore be merciful, just as your Father also is merciful. (Luke 6:35–36)

> For He makes His sun rise on the evil and on the good, and sends rain on the just and on the unjust. (Mt. 5:45b)

We may think we are pretty good at being kind, until we get to thinking about being kind to those who are unkind to us. Seriously? After what she did? You want me to be kind to her? Yes. That's gospel kindness. Everything else falls short. We are to pray that God will bless our enemies. We are to return good for evil. This is gospel kindness. God always enables us to obey His commands. So when we run out of love or kindness, we must go to God and ask Him to give us fresh supplies of love. Then we are extending His love, not our own weak, watered-down version.

THE GOSPEL IS GOD'S KINDNESS DISPLAYED TO THE WORLD.

> But when *the kindness* and the love of God our Savior toward man appeared . . . . (Tit. 3:4)

> . . . that in the ages to come He might show the exceeding riches of his grace in *His kindness* toward us in Christ Jesus. (Eph. 2:7)

The ultimate kindness to our fallen world was the arrival of a Savior. He came at great cost to Himself to redeem a race of sinners. That is a kindness that is indescribable. There is nothing like it on earth.

GOD ENABLES US TO BE KIND.

"But the fruit of the Spirit is . . . kindness" (Gal. 5:22). God bestows His Holy Spirit on His people and fills them. This results in fruit, the kind of fruit we could never produce on our own. Then, after giving us His kindness, He commands us to share it, extending it to others. So we really can't take credit for any kindness we extend to others, but we should give God all the glory and the thanks.

GOD COMMANDS US TO BE KIND.

"And *be kind* to one another, tenderhearted, forgiving one another, even as God in Christ forgave you" (Eph. 4:32).

This is the verse my husband's mother made all her kids memorize. Children must learn to be kind!

"Therefore, as the elect of God, holy and beloved, put on tender mercies, *kindness*, humility, meekness, longsuffering" (Col. 3:12). Kindness is something we "put on" by faith. We choose to put it on like we would put on a coat.

Notice below in the list of virtues we are to add to our faith (2 Pet. 1:7), we are to include brotherly kindness. You see the family connection here: it is *brotherly* kindness.

> But also for this very reason, giving all diligence, add to your faith virtue, to virtue knowledge, to knowledge self-control, to self-control perseverance, to perseverance godliness, to godliness *brotherly kindness*, and to brotherly kindness love. For if these things are yours and abound, you will be neither barren nor unfruitful in the knowledge of our Lord Jesus Christ. (2 Pet. 1:5–8)

> Love suffers long and is *kind*. (1 Cor. 13:4a)

> Be *kindly affectionate* to one another with *brotherly love*, in honor giving preference to one another. (Rom. 12:10)

If you have a close, affectionate family, you understand the description here of brotherly love. But if you have a family with little love for one another, then the comparison is lost on you. But that is all the more reason for you to draw near to God and ask Him to teach you what this looks like. The Christian church is compared to a family and a body. We are to be like a big, affectionate family.

A Few Traits of Kindness

- Kindness expresses itself. It is affectionate!
- Kindness is quick to forgive.
- Kindness is tender.
- Kindness is humble.
- Kindness is patient.
- Kindness honors others and doesn't look for honor for itself.

Examples of Kindness in the New Testament

> And the natives showed us unusual kindness; for they kindled a fire and made us all welcome, because of the rain that was falling and because of the cold. (Acts 28:2)

Hospitality is a way of showing kindness to strangers. Paul was shipwrecked on an island, and the native people there provided a warm fire and welcomed the poor, shipwrecked (no doubt bedraggled), hungry castaways. Not only that, but this was a boatload of criminals! Verse 42: "And the soldiers' plan was to kill the prisoners, lest any of them should swim away and escape.

And the next day we landed at Sidon. And Julius treated Paul kindly and gave him liberty to go to his friends and receive care" (Acts 27:3).

In Acts 27 Paul is a prisoner, but his guard made sure he could have fellowship with his friends and receive help from them. There are many ways to show kindness. We are to take all our opportunities and offer them to the Lord. He always blesses kindness when it is done in His name. "For whoever gives you a cup of water to drink in My name, because you belong to Christ, assuredly, I say to you, he will by no means lose his reward" (Mk. 9:41).

Kind Words

We also have the example of the Proverbs 31 woman, who has the *law of kindness* on her tongue: "She opens her mouth with wisdom, and on her tongue is the law of kindness" (Prov. 31:26).

Notice that kindness is a law. That means kindness guides and governs our actions. Many of your mother's "laws" are for your safety, both body and soul. They are kind laws.

Kindness is often demonstrated by kind words as well as kind actions. What is a kind word? Something that expresses compassion, sympathy, affection, encouragement, or friendliness.

Kind Actions

Kind actions are those that go beyond mere duty. They give more than what is required. We call that going the extra mile. A few examples would include making a meal, giving a ride, visiting the sick, writing a note, taking care of kids, cleaning up a mess, volunteering to help. There are many, many more ways to be kind.

Hindrances

This all sounds so good. What ever could hinder us from just overflowing with kindness all the time?

1. Bitterness and resentment chokes out kindness. If you are keeping a record of wrongs, then you believe that the person doesn't deserve your kindness. But if it is based on our worthiness, then no one deserves kindness.
2. Selfishness is too busy to be kind. You are too preoccupied with your own schedule that you can't be bothered.
3. Reciprocity. "Maybe I would be kind if someone was kind to me." This is kindness with a price tag. "I will give to this person if they will return the favor."
4. Shyness or timidity. But shyness can be a poor excuse. It turns out that shyness is sometimes actually rudeness or selfishness.

5. Shirking. This is when you think that someone else will do it because you just don't want to.

ꕥ QUESTIONS ꕥ

1. Think of a special kindness you received. What made it memorable?

2. Some people are so thoughtful. How can we imitate them?

3. There is always a temptation to get credit for kindness. How do we resist it?

4. What holds us back from being kind to some people?

10

LOYALTY

Loyalty, or steadfastness, is a form of faithfulness. It means following through on your commitments, promises, and obligations. A wife promises to be loyal to her husband when she takes her wedding vows "till death do us part." Her married life is to be a living out of these promises. In the same way, a Christian is called to be firmly loyal, following Christ to the end, not changing like the wind.

God is sure, dependable, reliable, constant, and unwavering. He never changes. He will never leave us or forsake us (Heb. 13:5). We are to imitate Him in this as in everything else. When we choose to be loyal to Christ, it follows that we will be loyal to our family and friends and to the body of Christ.

We choose our loyalties.

"No one can serve two masters; for either he will hate the one and love the other, or else he will be *loyal* to the one and despise the other. You cannot serve God and mammon" (Mt. 6:24). Jesus makes it clear that we cannot love both God and the world. The Christian must forsake the world and follow Christ. You cannot serve two masters. We must take up our cross and follow Him.

Demas is a good example here. "For Demas has forsaken me, having loved this present world" (2 Tim. 4:10a). He left Paul because he loved the world. And notice the word "present" that describes the world. The world is going to fade away! It is here now, and it can distract us, but what a foolish thing it is to leave what is eternal (God) for what is present (the world).

The world hates God.

The world hates Christ, and so it will hate His followers. This should not surprise us, because we "are not of the world" now that we are Christians.

"If you were of the world, the world would love its own. Yet because you are not of the world, but I chose you out of the world, therefore the world hates you" (Jn. 15:19). When we understand the world rightly, we can see how foolish we are to be distracted by it. If we want to follow Christ, the world will hate us. If we want the world to love us, God will hate us. That's what it boils down to. Which will it be? "For what profit is it to a man if he gains the whole world, and loses his own soul? Or what will a man give in exchange for his soul?" (Mt. 16:26).

Don't love the world!

> Adulterers and adulteresses! Do you not know that friendship with the world is enmity with God? Whoever therefore wants to be a friend of the world makes himself an enemy of God. (Jas. 4:4)

> Do not love the world or the things in the world. If anyone loves the world, the love of the Father is not in him. (1 Jn. 2:15)

> And do not be conformed to this world, but be transformed by the renewing of your mind, that you may prove what is that good and acceptable and perfect will of God. (Rom. 12:2)

We are at war with the world. That is why Christian women should not adopt the uniform of the enemy. We should not look the way the world wants us to look, or dress the way the world dictates, or live to gain the world's approval. This is antithetical to our faith.

Jesus is steadfast.

"Now before the Feast of the Passover, when Jesus knew that His hour had come that He should depart from this world to the Father, having loved His own who were in the world, *He loved them to the end*" (Jn. 13:1). Jesus was loyal to his disciples, and He continues to be. If we are His own, we can know for sure that He will love us to the end. This is a tremendous consolation. The world is fickle. Those who are in the world's favor today are out-of-favor tomorrow. Jesus, on the other hand, is constant.

Steadfastness is a matter of the heart.

> My heart is *steadfast*, O God, my heart is *steadfast*; I will sing and give praise. (Ps. 57:7)

> He will not be afraid of evil tidings; His heart is *steadfast*, trusting in the Lord. (Ps. 112:7)

Steadfastness is internal; it is a heart attitude. Notice that a steadfast heart sings, praises, is not afraid, and trusts the

Lord. Even when bad news arrives, a steadfast heart hangs on because God is faithful.

Steadfastness is stubborn.

"Therefore, my beloved brethren, *be steadfast*, immovable, always abounding in the work of the Lord, knowing that your labor is not in vain in the Lord" (1 Cor. 15:58).

A steadfast heart cannot be moved. It is the best kind of stubborn! And what is it stubborn about? A steadfast heart is taken up with the Lord's work.

Warnings to Be Steadfast

> . . . if indeed you continue in the faith, grounded and *steadfast*, and are not moved away from the hope of the gospel which you heard, which was preached to every creature under heaven, of which I, Paul, became a minister. (Col. 1:23)

> For we have become partakers of Christ if we hold the beginning of our confidence *steadfast* to the end. (Heb. 3:14)

> You therefore, beloved, since you know this beforehand, beware lest you also fall from your own *steadfastness*, being led away with the error of the wicked; but grow in the grace and knowledge of our Lord and Savior Jesus Christ. To Him be the glory both now and forever. Amen. (2 Pet. 3:17–18)

These verses warn us that we can move away or be led away or fall away from the faith. So what do we do about that? Be steadfast! We are to continue in the faith, be grounded in the faith, hold to our confidence, and grow in grace.

Steadfastness protects us from sin.

> Nevertheless they flattered Him with their mouth, and they lied to Him with their tongue; For their heart was *not steadfast* with Him, nor were they faithful in His covenant. (Ps. 78:36–37)

> Resist him [your adversary the devil], *steadfast* in the faith. (1 Pet. 5:9)

A steadfast heart is not moved by flatterers or liars, and is in a position of strength to resist the devil. Imagine how quickly the disloyal will give way to temptation.

Steadfastness is a cause of joy.

"For though I am absent in the flesh, yet I am with you in spirit, rejoicing to see your good order and the steadfastness of your faith in Christ" (Col. 2:5). Paul rejoices that the Colossians are steadfast in their faith. What a blessing it is to others when they see that we are stubbornly loyal to Jesus Christ. It encourages them and gives them cause to be loyal as well.

Run the race!

"Therefore we also, since we are surrounded by so great a cloud of witnesses, let us lay aside every weight, and the sin which so easily ensnares us, and let us run with endurance the race that is set before us, looking unto Jesus, the author and finisher of our faith" (Heb. 12:1–2a). Many men and women have laid their lives down for the gospel's sake. They have stood steadfast to the end and have gained their reward. This is what loyalty and steadfastness mean.

When we remember that He is the author and finisher of our faith, and that "He who has begun a good work in you will complete it until the day of Jesus Christ" (Phil. 1:6), we can pluck up our courage and keep running the race before us. "This hope we have as an anchor of the soul, both sure and *steadfast*" (Heb. 6:19a).

QUESTIONS

1. How can you demonstrate your loyalty to Christ in your relationships to people (your parents, husband, siblings, or friends)?

2. What are some of the common temptations to be disloyal?

3. How can you resist those temptations?

4. Can you think of how women in their teens are commonly tempted to be disloyal to their parents or Christian friends?

5. How can you recognize in yourself when you are not being steadfast?

11

CHASTITY

Chastity is a virtue we don't hear much about today because we live in an age of much open promiscuity, immorality, and impurity. This is all the more reason for Christian women to love to be chaste and pure, obeying God's Word rather than following the mad crowd.

"Chaste" means not participating in any sexual activity that is prohibited. But, you might ask, what exactly is prohibited in the world today? Pretty much anything goes. We are not looking to what our culture allows, but rather what God approves. He prohibits fornication and adultery and homosexuality. So even if our civil authorities permit or encourage such things, God doesn't. And He is our Maker. His authority is far above that of any civil authority. His law never changes, even when our culture is throwing off all restraint.

So, to be chaste is to be sexually pure, modest, and decent in our thoughts, words, and actions. Chastity is about keeping yourself sexually pure whether you are married or unmarried. An unmarried woman keeps herself from actions or thoughts that are not in keeping with protecting and honoring her virginity. A married woman is committed to sexual faithfulness to her husband. Marital fidelity is keeping the vows that are made at the wedding and obeying God's commands. In both cases, chaste women do not dress or behave or talk like a harlot. They are sexually pure.

You might want to ask just what qualifies as seductive or impure. When a married woman has an adulterous relationship, our culture calls it an "affair," which might sound nice and tidy. But we all know it's called cheating on your husband. The adulteress described in Proverbs shows us what kind of behavior we can call seductive or impure.

1. She is a smooth talker.

"For the lips of an immoral woman drip honey, and her mouth is smoother than oil; but in the end she is bitter as wormwood, sharp as a two-edged sword. Her feet go down to death, her steps lay hold of hell" (Prov. 5:3–5).

2. She is attractive, and uses her eyes to send a seductive invitation.
"Reproofs of instruction are the way of life, to keep you from the evil woman, from the flattering tongue of a seductress. Do not lust after her beauty in your heart, nor let her allure you with her eyelids. For by means of a harlot a man is reduced to a crust of bread; and an adulteress will prey upon his precious life" (Prov. 6:23b–26).

3. She is out in public where she might find a likely target. She dresses provocatively. She is mouthy, and she likes to break the rules.
"And there a woman met him, with the attire of a harlot, and a crafty heart. She was loud and rebellious. Her feet would not stay at home" (Prov. 7:10–11).

4. She flirts and entices and flatters.
"With her enticing speech she caused him to yield, with her flattering lips she seduced him" (Prov. 7:21).

Some of this flirting and flattering conduct can be carried on today on social media. Foolish women put up suggestive photos of themselves and have private conversations with men they don't know very well or don't know at all. Remember, her path leads to hell.

And let's be honest here. Many films today have sluts and whores as the central protagonists. The audience is manipulated into thinking they are sweet or honorable or honest or courageous or kind. But the truth is they portray fornicators and adulteresses. They should not be role models for any women who want to be chaste. They dress immodestly, they speak and act immodestly, and they commit fornication casually. If we want to be chaste women, we will not be entertained by such things.

Chastity is not just for the unmarried.

All Christian women, of all ages, whether married, unmarried, or widowed, are called to be chaste. But sexual purity is not the same thing as prudishness. God intends for marriage between a man and a woman to picture Christ and the Church. The one flesh of married sexual union is good and right and pure. But all sexual unions outside of marriage are shameful and sinful and unclean. What God created to be holy and honorable for marriage is dishonorable outside of marriage. So when we have a high view of marriage, we will have a corresponding high view of sexual purity. Sexual purity is for women, and it is for men. God does not have different standards for men and women.

> That they admonish the young women to love their husbands, to love their children, to be discreet, *chaste*, homemakers, good, obedient to their own husbands, that the word of God may not be blasphemed. (Tit. 2:4–5)

> Marriage is honorable among all, and the bed undefiled; but fornicators and adulterers God will judge. (Heb. 13:4)

Virginity Until Marriage

Virginity is a physical fact, but it should also be a spiritual reality. Some women think that so long as they don't have sexual intercourse, everything else is okay. They may be technically virgins, but they have lost their purity and virginity in other ways. Purity means staying free from all sexual activity until marriage. It means keeping your heart and mind free from lust. "For I am jealous for you with godly jealousy. For I have betrothed you to one husband, that I may present you as a *chaste* virgin to Christ. But I fear, lest somehow, as the serpent deceived Eve by his craftiness, so your minds may be corrupted from the simplicity that is in Christ" (2 Cor. 11:2–3).

Forgiveness

Our good God forgives all sin, including sexual sins of fornication, adultery, homosexuality, and impurity. He is gracious and merciful and puts our sins far from us in the Cross of Christ. But we should not presume on His grace and make plans to sin that we can confess later. This just leads to regret. Confess your sins honestly and thank God for His forgiveness. And then "Keep yourself pure" (1 Tim. 5:22b).

Fidelity after Marriage

A Christian wife must be faithful to her husband. That means she should not cultivate close friendships with men who are not her husband. Even if she has no evil intentions, she can set herself up for temptations. Women are commonly seduced emotionally before they are seduced physically. They allow themselves to become too close to someone who is not their husband, and then the friendship swings into a physical relationship that is adulterous. This is how a woman can tear her house down with her own hands. There is never good fruit from adultery. It is right up there in the ten commandments.

God's Will

If you think chastity is just a suggestion for Christian men and women, you are confused. All Christians are to live chaste lives in all generations. This has always been God's command, purpose, and plan.

> For this is the will of God, your sanctification: that you should abstain from sexual immorality; that each of you should know how to possess his own vessel in sanctification and honor, not in passion of lust, like the Gentiles who do not know God; that no one should take advantage of and defraud his brother in this matter, because the Lord is the avenger of all such, as we also forewarned you and testified. For God did not call us to uncleanness, but in holiness. (1 Thess. 4:3–7)

God Will Judge It

God blesses obedience and judges sin. We cannot live sexually impure lives and look for God's blessing. Sexual sin is destructive and brings misery with it.

> For this you know, that no fornicator, unclean person, nor covetous man, who is an idolater, has any inheritance in the kingdom of Christ and God. (Eph. 5:5)

> Lest there be any fornicator or profane person like Esau, who for one morsel of food sold his birthright. (Heb. 12:16)

QUESTIONS

1. What sorts of things can cause mental uncleanness?

2. Do you indulge in sexually impure movies or books or jokes?

3. What is the Christian standard for sexual behavior?

4. How is sexual purity at war with our culture?

5. How can you take precautions against sexual sin?

12

MODESTY

Modesty is a natural outworking of many of these virtues we have been studying. It is the result or manifestation of having a chaste heart. And it is also the result of many of the other virtues we have studied so far. For example, we need wisdom and prudence as we make choices about clothing. Contentment keeps us from the temptation to competition (which drives much immodesty). And so all these virtues weave together nicely. "In like manner also, that the women adorn themselves in modest apparel, with propriety and moderation, not with braided hair or gold or costly clothing, but, which is proper for women professing godliness, with good works" (1 Tim. 2:9–10).

The previous passage is clearly addressing the sticky subject of clothing, so let's look first at what modest clothing is; then we will look at what it isn't.

Propriety

You should not wear your nightgown and flip flops to the grocery story. That would not be appropriate. So *propriety* refers to what is suitable for the occasion. Modest apparel is clothing that conforms to the Christian standards of good behavior or manners. In this sense, we dress for the sake of others, to be courteous to them.

Moderation

We sometimes think that if one is good, then two must be better, but that is not always the case. A large hot pink hat with ostrich feathers worn to a wedding might distract everyone's attention away from the bride. So moderation means showing some restraint and choosing something less showy, less extreme, a little quieter. Something that won't steal the show or draw undue attention to you and away from others of more importance. Moderation is humble.

Pretentiousness

Modest clothing by definition can't be pretentious. Pretentious clothes show off the brand or the price. They are self-important clothes. See how this is at war with virtue? Humility can't dress up to look like pride because that is not in its nature. So often, women are wanting to impress one another with their appearance. But modesty is thinking more about others. It's not putting on airs.

Extravagance

This is the opposite of moderation. Extravagance often has to do with the price, and Paul specifically mentions that Christian women shouldn't go for the "gold or pearls or costly clothing." If we are thinking of moderation, we won't spend an excessive amount of money on decking ourselves out. In other words, we are not wasteful.

Modesty isn't about rules.

So often we want a list of rules about modesty, and we think only in terms of how much skin is exposed. But the Bible is coming at modesty a different way. God wants us to think in His terms. Now when we do this, it will certainly affect how much of our body we reveal. But we don't start there.

We start with a chaste heart that is sexually pure, which means we will already have strong opinions of our own about how tight or how low or how short our clothes will be. This is so we can move on from those considerations to other, more weighty issues.

Proper

Our dress says a lot about us, and God wants our outside to reflect what is in the inside. So modesty for Christian women must be connected to what is proper or right for a godly woman to wear. That word *proper* is connected to *propriety* and *appropriate.* If you are a godly Christian woman, it would be inconsistent to wear something improper or at war with the reality of your godliness. Your dress should be a good fit with your character. You dress like a godly woman because you are a godly woman. But then we might come back to the old problem: but what is "proper" for a godly Christian woman? "Can you give me a list?"

Good Works

Here's the list we've been looking for: good works. We are to adorn ourselves with good works. This seems like Paul is changing the subject entirely. He is just getting warmed up to making rules about braids and pearls and stuff, but then he bails. But he didn't: Paul wants Christian women who profess godliness to keep their priorities straight, and he knows how much we are interested in clothing and jewelry and hair and the rest. He wants us to govern our desire to look pretty (which is not a bad thing in itself) by keeping our priority on the good works God has planned for us to walk in. If we keep our interest in clothing in perspective, behind good works, we will see that good works are far prettier, fit us better, and please God more.

Application

But we seldom really apply this. We spend our time trying to figure out how short, how low, and how tight we can go rather than actually applying this verse. If we are honest with ourselves, we have to confess that we often want people to notice our clothes more than our good works. But if that is the case, then we are not dressing in clothing that is proper for women professing godliness. We might try to wear clothing that is not too short, too low, or too tight, and we think we've nailed modesty. But we are still looking for approval for what we are wearing. We still are looking for attention and affirmation by dressing to please the crowd. And that is not modest. The heart of modesty is good works.

So try this. When you get into your closet to find something to wear, think about putting on good works. Wear something that is appropriate and moderate. Keep the volume turned down. And then get down to the real business of doing good works.

Modesty is beautiful.

Modesty underscores beauty. It turns out that if we dress modestly and turn our attention to good works, we will grow more beautiful. Obedience is always blessed with fruit, and fruit beautifies.

QUESTIONS

1. What are some of the "rules" for modesty you have adopted or others have adopted for you?

2. How would your own wardrobe be affected if you were thinking in terms of propriety and moderation when you shop?

3. How do some women take "modesty" to an extreme? Is that moderation?

4. What are some of the good deeds you can put on today?

13
GRATITUDE

Gratitude is the Christian's first and highest duty. We are created to be a grateful people, returning thanks to our God in and for all things. Consider this small sampling of verses from the Psalms:

> It is good to give *thanks* to the Lord, and to sing praises to Your name, O Most High. (Ps. 92:1)

> Enter into His gates with *thanksgiving*, and into His courts with praise. Be thankful to Him, and bless His name. (Ps. 100:4)

> Let us come before His presence with *thanksgiving*; let us shout joyfully to Him with psalms. (Ps. 95:2)

> That I may proclaim with the voice of *thanksgiving*, and tell of all Your wondrous works. (Ps. 26:7)

Thanksgiving is something that should characterize our lives every day. This is one of the distinctives of the Christian faith—because we have Someone to thank. When an atheist says that he is grateful, I wonder to whom he is grateful. All gratitude has to end up at God's feet. If an atheist feels gratitude for his health or his parents or his job or his life, who gave it all to him? Gratitude has to have an object! So thanksgiving is a way of life for the Christian. We have all His wondrous works to praise Him for, and that will give us plenty of material every day to fill our hearts with thanksgiving. And it is good to give thanks. It is good for our souls to praise our Creator.

It's wonderful that our country still celebrates a day called Thanksgiving. We feast appropriately and take the day off from work and school. Some want to call it Turkey Day instead of Thanksgiving, which is a very lame substitute! But I have to think that those behind "Turkey Day" understand that we must render thanks to Someone, and they don't want to do it. Thanksgiving is a Christian holiday because we are the only people who worship our Maker the way He has told us to in His Word.

When? What?

The Christian expresses thanks *for all things* to God *always.*

> . . .but be filled with the Spirit, speaking to one another in psalms and hymns and spiritual songs, singing and making melody in your heart to the Lord, giving *thanks* always for all things to God the Father in the name of the Lord Jesus Christ, submitting to one another in the fear of God. (Eph. 5:18b–21)

This makes sense because we know all things are under God's control. So we can be thankful that the world is not just a bunch of random things happening with no overarching purpose, but rather a well executed plan governed by an all-powerful and entirely good God.

Gratitude Versus Worry

Anxiety is a common sin, and the clear way to resist the temptation to worry is to lay our concerns and troubles out to God in prayer, with thankful hearts. The presence of thanksgiving is a sign of our faith. When we do this, God's peace protects our hearts and minds from anxious thoughts. "Be anxious for nothing, but in everything by prayer and supplication, with *thanksgiving*, let your requests be made known to God; and the peace of God, which surpasses all understanding, will guard your hearts and minds through Christ Jesus" (Phil. 4:6–7).

Women are called to have a "gentle and quiet spirit" in 1 Peter 3:4. This is a spirit that is resting in God's faithfulness and trusting Him. It does not mean it is a woman who doesn't speak. Her spirit is not troubled by anxieties and cares, so her spirit is quiet. If we cover our prayers and thoughts with thanksgiving, we will please God. If we give way to anxious thoughts, this results in turbulent spirits and that leads to complaining and arguing. The contentious woman is described in Proverbs as a drippy faucet who drives others to take refuge in the wilderness (Prov. 21:19; 27:15).

Our Prayers

"Continue earnestly in prayer, being vigilant in it with *thanksgiving*" (Col. 4:2). We are to pour our hearts out to God in prayer with regularity, not occasionally. *Earnestly* means we are giving ourselves seriously to prayer and with sincerity of heart. *Vigilant* means we are alert and attentive in our prayers and not praying casually or carelessly, but giving ourselves to it with true diligence. And all with thanksgiving! "Oh, give thanks to the Lord! Call upon His name; make known His deeds among the peoples!" (Ps. 105:1).

UNGRATEFUL

"Because, although they knew God, they did not glorify Him as God, nor were thankful, but became futile in their thoughts, and their foolish hearts were darkened" (Rom. 1:21). Unregenerate men know there is a God, even if they claim to be atheist or agnostic. The heavens declare the glory of God loud and clear, day-in and day-out. So the unbelievers have no excuse. We see here in Romans 1 that they choose not to glorify or thank God, and the result of this ingratitude is dark hearts and futile minds. The way out of their spiritual darkness is to repent and believe. When we look at the hard hearts of sinful men and women, we see a stubborn refusal to acknowledge their Creator.

But Christians can be ungrateful as well. Do you ever complain about the weather? Who ordained it? Or about getting up in the morning when the alarm goes off? Or about the little things in your day that didn't go as planned? Who ordained those? (Ouch!) These are common ways we dishonor God. Ingratitude hardens and darkens. Gratitude enlarges and enlivens.

THANKSGIVING IS A GOOD CHOICE.

As with all the other virtues, when we practice this by faith, we please God and we glorify Him and we become more like Him as a result. And our faith grows. And this is good. But how do we get there?

1. Confess ingratitude as sin. Thank Him for His forgiveness.
2. Ask God to show you where you've been complaining, and confess those sins as well.
3. Make a list of the things for which you are very grateful, and thank God for each item on your list.
4. Make a list of the hard things in your life, the troubles and trials. Now thank God for each one.
5. Make a list of the hard people in your life, and thank God for each one of those as well.
6. Now you are in a position to thank God for all His wondrous works because you have removed the ingratitude and the complaining.
7. Pray that God will help you express gratitude for all things all the time.

QUESTIONS

1. What are common ways we neglect to be thankful?

2. How can you express gratitude besides in your prayers?

3. How should we react when we are around others who are grumbling and complaining?

4. What hinders us from being a more thankful people?

14
DOMESTICITY

Since this is a book about virtue, it's of special note that the woman of Proverbs 31 is first singled out as *virtuous*. "Who can find a virtuous wife? For her worth is far above rubies" (Prov. 31:10). The next twenty verses describe her in the context of her domestic duties, at which she excels. Domesticity is a broad field and encompasses all of life in the home. But let's look at what this chapter in Proverbs specifically identifies as domestic arts and duties.

The Domestic Arts

From the following collection of verses, we see that this woman is very talented and capable: she spins and weaves, she shops and cooks, she buys real estate and plants a vineyard, she sells her handmade goods, she is generous to the poor, she sews nice clothing for herself, and she is a fabric and clothing designer.

> She seeks wool and flax, and willingly works with her hands. (v. 13)

> She is like the merchant ships, she brings her food from afar. She also rises while it is yet night, and provides food for her household. (vv. 14–15a)

> She considers a field and buys it; From her profits she plants a vineyard. (v. 16)

> She perceives that her merchandise is good. (v. 18a)

> She stretches out her hands to the distaff, and her hand holds the spindle. (v. 19)

> She extends her hands to the poor, yes, she reaches out her hands to the needy. (v. 20)

> She makes tapestry for herself; her clothing is fine linen and purple. (v. 22)

> She makes linen garments and sells them, and supplies sashes for the merchants. (v. 24)

This woman may seem rather intimidating and so we ask, "Do we have to do all these things?" This is not a to-do list, but a description of a woman who is clearly enjoying herself. She is flourishing and prospering and using her particular gifts, resources, and opportunities. We each have our own homes, our own gifts, and our own resources and opportunities. The key is to be investing ourselves and our talents in our homes with creativity and joy, and not to feel "burdened" to produce something comparable to this woman in Proverbs.

The Domestic Attitude

Gathering more examples from this chapter of Proverbs, let's consider not *what* she does, but *how* she does it.

1. She works willingly (v. 13). She is a go-getter and doesn't need prompting or reminding or urging.
2. She is not afraid of working hard. "She girds herself with strength, and strengthens her arms" (v. 17). She is not a weakling, but a strong woman. She does not shrink back from hard work.
3. She has a generous spirit (v. 20) and is looking out for the needy.

4. "She is not afraid of snow for her household" (v. 21). She has planned ahead and anticipated needs. She is not caught off guard by predictable things like winter.
5. Joy characterizes this woman's work: "She shall rejoice in time to come" (v. 25).
6. "She opens her mouth with wisdom, and on her tongue is the law of kindness" (v. 26). A homemaker has to lay down the law in many areas. It may be firm, but it is kind, and delivered with wisdom.
7. "She watches over the ways of her household, and does not eat the bread of idleness" (v. 27). She is eager to get to work and is not wasting time.
8. "A woman who fears the Lord, she shall be praised" (v. 30). This is the bottom line. All of these "doings" come from "being" the kind of woman who fears and worships God.

To Sum Up

She does good, seeks, works, brings, rises, provides, considers, plants, girds, strengthens, perceives, stretches, extends, reaches out, is not afraid, makes, sells, supplies, rejoices, opens, watches, and fears the Lord. There is not one negative thing in this whole section. She sounds like a woman who would be fun to know and watch. I've known women like this who were powerhouses and never seemed to run out of inspiration or energy. But I also know many quiet women who are just as productive, but most of it is behind the scenes. We use the strengths and personalities God has given us to glorify Him where we are and with what we have been given. That's why no two homes will be exactly alike.

Manage Your Home

> Therefore I desire that the younger widows marry, bear children, *manage the house*, give no opportunity to the adversary to speak reproachfully. (1 Tim. 5:14)

> She watches over the ways of her *household*, and does not eat the bread of idleness. (Prov. 31:27)

Managing a home is a big job that requires skill and diligence. If we want to change the world one home at a time, then we have to start by taking dominion of our own homes. If you don't have a home of your own, but just a room of your own, then you can start there. What does your room look like? Are you being faithful with a little? If not, then why should God give you more? We can only export what we have. If our homes are joyful and beautiful, then we have something to share. But if they are disorganized and slovenly, we are not yet ready.

The Center of the Home

"Your wife shall be like a fruitful vine in the very heart of your house, your children like olive plants all around your table" (Ps. 128:3). The wife is the very heart of the home. She holds a central position which God has given her. She is a source of great blessing.

Notice what else is central in this home: the table. The kids are all gathered around the table with eager, hungry faces! This picture should help us see how God values table fellowship. Our tables are a shadow or picture of the Lord's Table, where we take the wine and the bread together. This means hard work, joyful preparation, and sacrifice. "She is like the merchant ships, she brings her food from afar" (Prov. 31:14).

Make Your Home

> The wise woman *builds her house,* But the foolish pulls it down with her hands. (Prov. 14:1)

> That they admonish the young women to love their husbands, to love their children, to be discreet, chaste, *homemakers*, good,

> obedient to their own husbands, that the word of God may not be blasphemed. (Tit. 2:4–5)

God is our Maker, and we are makers, imitating Him. A homemaker is a woman who is making her home. Not only does she *make* her home, but she *loves* her home. She is taking dominion. She is devoted to her family. She studies and manages the affairs of her home and enjoys her calling. She is farsighted. She understands that her home is a building block in that big project called Christendom. Without Christian homes, there can be no Christian culture.

Fill Your Home

"Through wisdom a *house* is built and by understanding it is established; by knowledge the rooms are filled with all precious and pleasant riches" (Prov. 24:3–4). I hope you see that building and furnishing and filling a home is a great privilege. It is a gift! A virtuous woman is going to fill her home with pleasant things—hot meals and stories and gifts and laughter and work and messes and clean-up and toys and children and songs. These are precious riches that money can't buy. A woman who fears God provides stability, comfort, beauty, and order in her home. This is a tall order and requires faith, hard work, and a vivid imagination.

QUESTIONS

1. What skills does a homemaker need today?

2. What are some of the domestic arts that you would like to pursue? How can you do this?

3. How does our culture view the homemaker?

4. How do you view a career in homemaking?

5. If you are not yet married, how are you preparing for homemaking?

6. Home life is always changing. What are some of the challenges you are facing at this stage? How can you approach these challenges with faith?

7. Why does a homemaker need a vivid imagination?

15

PATIENCE

Patience is one of those virtues that we all want, but we don't really want to have to exercise too much. Patience means "putting up with" suffering or pain, provocation of all kinds, delays when we are in a hurry, unforeseen difficulties, unexpected interruptions, insults or unkindness, all manner of troubles and confusion. Patience can bear up under these circumstances with calmness and self-control. Patience refuses to be provoked or angered, and can quietly press on without complaining. And all of this for a long time.

One of the other terms for patience is longsuffering. This word is not too tricky to figure out. It quite simply means suffering for a long time. Add to that, suffering for a long time *with joy.* Let's all be honest here: this is quite clearly impossible without God's intervening grace! But He does give us grace. And so we begin by looking to Him.

God's Patience

> But you, O Lord, are a God full of compassion, and gracious, *longsuffering* and abundant in mercy and truth. (Ps. 86:15)

> For whatever things were written before were written for our learning, that we through the *patience* and comfort of the Scriptures might have hope. Now may the God of *patience* and comfort grant you to be like-minded toward one another, according to Christ Jesus. (Rom. 15:4–5)

The Scriptures give us patience and comfort, which in turn give us hope. In his exposition of these verses, Matthew Henry says that the Scriptures are the "conduit pipe," but God is the fountainhead: "The more patience and comfort we receive from God, the better disposed we are to love one another. Nothing breaks the peace more than an impatient, and peevish, and fretful melancholy temper."

He exhibits patience toward us.

"However, for this reason I obtained mercy, that in me first Jesus Christ might show all longsuffering, as a pattern to those who are going to believe on Him for everlasting life" (1 Tim. 1:16). Paul points out that God was longsuffering towards him during that time when he was persecuting the church.

And He is longsuffering toward those whom He will judge.

" . . .who formerly were disobedient, when once the Divine longsuffering waited in the days of Noah, while the ark was being prepared . . ." (1 Pet. 3:20a). God does not judge in haste, but waits for His own good timing.

Flee and Pursue.

"But you, O man of God, flee these things and pursue righteousness, godliness, faith, love, patience, gentleness" (1 Tim. 6:11). The Bible often gives us a list of things to stop doing and a list of things to start doing. It is rather like pulling up weeds and planting flowers. Just planting flowers among the weeds is not wise, and if we pull up the weeds, we need to replace them with something positive. Otherwise, the weeds just fill in again. In the previous verses, Timothy is told to run away from the love of money and greed and foolish and harmful lusts. Those are the weeds. And he is told to plant (pursue) good things, including patience. "But the fruit of the spirit is love, joy, peace, longsuffering…" (Gal. 5:22).

Galatians 5 has a list of the works of the flesh that is exhibited by those who will not inherit eternal life. This is followed by a list of the fruit of the Spirit. Patience or longsuffering is not a natural ability but a work of the Spirit. You should not be discouraged if you are not naturally a patient person. You should pursue it. Chase it down. Look for opportunities to be patient. Pray for opportunities to be patient. And in the midst of the trial, pray for patience and thank God for His patience working in you.

Patient with all.

"Now we exhort you, brethren, warn those who are unruly, comfort the fainthearted, uphold the weak, be patient with all" (1 Thess. 5:14). Patient with whom? All. This includes the unruly, the fainthearted, and the weak. In other words, we are to be patient with everyone with whom we might be tempted to become impatient.

Joyful patience in trials.

> My brethren, count it all joy when you fall into various trials, knowing that the testing of your faith produces patience. But

> let patience have its perfect work, that you may be perfect and complete, lacking nothing. (Jas. 1:2–4)

> [Be] patient in tribulation. (Rom. 12:12)

> For what credit is it if, when you are beaten for your faults, you take it patiently? But when you do good and suffer, if you take it patiently, this is commendable before God. (1 Pet. 2:20)

When we believe that all things really do work together for our good (Rom. 8:28), then we can trust that all our trials are from the hand of our loving Father. We can be patient in them because He is perfecting us, and trials are one of His most useful tools in this process.

Not only are we to be patient, but we are to count it all joy. This is the test of our faith. When we rejoice in the Lord, this produces the fruit of patience in our lives. Without joy, patience is just gritting our teeth and forcing ourselves to be patient. Joy is what identifies the patience as the real thing.

Joyful patience signals a worthy walk.

> I therefore, the prisoner of the Lord, beseech you to walk worthy of the calling with which you were called, with all lowliness and gentleness, with longsuffering, bearing with one another in love,

endeavoring to keep the unity of the Spirit in the bond of peace." (Eph. 4:1–3)

"That you may walk worthy of the Lord, fully pleasing Him, being fruitful in every good work and increasing in the knowledge of God; strengthened with all might, according to His glorious power, for all patience and longsuffering with joy." (Col. 1:10–11)

Two things here to note. First, patience is a sign that we are walking according to the calling we received in Christ. Second, joyful patience is a sign that we have been strengthened by the glorious power of God. There is no other explanation for it!

We are to wait patiently for God's deliverance.

Rest in the Lord, and wait patiently for Him; do not fret because of him who prospers in his way, because of the man who brings wicked schemes to pass. (Ps. 37:7)

Wait on the Lord; be of good courage, and He shall strengthen your heart; wait, I say, on the Lord! (Ps. 27:14)

But those who wait on the Lord shall renew their strength; they shall mount up with wings like eagles, they shall run and not be weary, they shall walk and not faint. (Isaiah 40:31)

When you are in a trouble, do not give up praying and waiting. God will answer in His good time. So we pray, we lay out our requests, we ask for deliverance, and we wait joyfully. To wait means that we continue to look forward with eager expectation. Waiting is a spiritual discipline. It is not something that the flesh does easily. We want to see an answer now. We want instant results so we can move on. But the Scripture is full of verses about waiting. And waiting some more.

> I waited patiently for the Lord; and He inclined to me, and heard my cry. (Ps. 40:1)

> It is good that one should hope and wait quietly for the salvation of the Lord. (Lam. 3:26)

We must rest as we wait, hope while we wait, be quiet while we wait, and wait patiently. How many of us are good at waiting? How many of us wait quietly, patiently, and hopefully? Or are we tapping our foot, watching the clock (or the calendar), and grumbling about how long this is taking?

Waiting on the Lord bears good fruit in us. Waiting results in renewal and fresh strength. Faithful waiting is watching expectantly, looking for the Lord to come with His answer any minute. Faithful watching keeps on waiting, knowing that waiting on the Lord is a good thing in itself. And waiting for the Lord is a means of getting His attention. "I'm still here, Lord. I'm still asking, watching, waiting patiently for You to act."

When we start to give up waiting, our hearts get hard. We become weak and weary. But the act of waiting in faith strengthens our faith. Then we can say with confidence, "Therefore I will look to the Lord; I will wait for the God of my salvation; My God will hear me" (Mic. 7:7).

QUESTIONS

1. In what areas (at home, school, work) do you need to exercise joyful patience?

2. Do you ever need to be patient with yourself?

3. Do others have to be patient with you?

4. Have you ever given up waiting on the Lord?

5. How can you resume waiting joyfully on the Lord?

CONCLUSION

Now that you have concluded this study, I hope you will continue to "add to your faith virtue." Virtues are good qualities that God wants His people to cultivate, and if I had added all the virtues I could find in the Bible, this little book would be much bigger than it is. For example, what about generosity? That's a wonderful virtue, so don't neglect it.

In our pursuit of holiness, we are pursuing God. We are imitating, loving, and following Him. Never forget that pursuing virtue is not about us, but about our good and gracious Father who loves to bestow the righteousness of Christ on us. All our days on this earth should be characterized by our desire to please and glorify Him, and that necessarily includes pursuing virtue.